iPad®

FOR

DUMMIES®

MINI EDITION

by Edward C. Baig

USA TODAY Personal Tech columnist

and

Bob LeVitus

Houston Chronicle "Dr. Mac" columnist

WILEY

Wiley Publishing, Inc.

iPad® For Dummies®, Mini Edition

Published by
Wiley Publishing, Inc.
111 River Street
Hoboken, NJ 07030-5774
www.wiley.com

Copyright © 2011 by Wiley Publishing, Inc., Indianapolis, Indiana

Published by Wiley Publishing, Inc., Indianapolis, Indiana

Published simultaneously in Canada

For general information on our other products and services, please contact our Customer Care Department within the U.S. at 877-762-2974, outside the U.S. at 317-572-3993, or fax 317-572-4002.

For technical support, please visit www.wiley.com/techsupport.

Wiley also publishes its books in a variety of electronic formats. Some content that appears in print may not be available in electronic books.

Mini Edition ISBN: 978-1-118-01185-0

Manufactured in the United States of America

WILEY

Contents at a Glance

Publisher's Acknowledgments

We're proud of this book; please send us your comments through our online registration form located at www.dummies.com/register/.

Some of the people who helped bring this book to market include the following:

Acquisitions and Editorial

Project Editor: Jodi Jensen

Executive Editor: Bob Woerner

Copy Editor: Brian Walls

Composition Services

Project Coordinator: Kristie Rees

Layout and Graphics: Samantha K. Cherolis

Publishing and Editorial for Technology Dummies

Richard Swadley, Vice President and Executive Group Publisher

Andy Cummings, Vice President and Publisher

Mary Bednarek, Executive Acquisitions Director

Mary C. Corder, Editorial Director

Publishing for Consumer Dummies

Diane Graves Steele, Vice President and Publisher

Composition Services

Debbie Stailey, Director of Composition Services

Introduction

• •

*A*s Yogi Berra would say, "It was déjà vu all over again": Front-page treatment, top billing on network TV and cable, and diehards lining up days in advance to ensure landing a highly lusted-after product from Apple. Like its revolutionary predecessors, the iPhone and the iPad, the iPad 2 is now hot indeed. But we trust you didn't pick up this book to read yet another account about how the iPad 2 launch was an epochal event. We trust you *did* buy the book to find out how to get the very most out of your remarkable device. Whether you have an iPad or the new iPad 2, our goal is to deliver that information in a light and breezy fashion.

About This Book

We think you're pretty darn smart for buying a *For Dummies* book. That says to us that you have the confidence and intelligence to know what you don't know. As with most Apple products, however, the iPad is beautifully designed and intuitive to use. You'll get pretty far just by exploring the iPad's many functions and features on your own, without the help of this (or any other) book. However, this book is chock-full of useful tips, advice, and other nuggets that should make your iPad experience all the more pleasurable.

Icons Used in This Book

Little round pictures (icons) appear in the left margins throughout this book. Consider these icons miniature road signs, telling you something extra about the topic at hand or hammering a point home.

Here's what the four icons used in this book look like and mean.

These are the juicy morsels, shortcuts, and recommendations that might make the task at hand faster or easier.

This icon emphasizes the stuff we think you ought to retain. You may even jot down a note to yourself in the iPad 2.

Put on your propeller beanie hat and pocket protector; this text includes the truly geeky stuff. You can safely ignore this material, but if it weren't interesting or informative, we wouldn't have bothered to write it.

You wouldn't intentionally run a stop sign, would you? In the same fashion, ignoring warnings may be hazardous to your iPad and (by extension) your wallet. There, you now know how these warning icons work, for you have just received your very first warning!

Part I

Introducing the iPad

Congratulations! With the iPad 2 you've selected an incredible device that combines a killer audio and video iPod, an e-book reader, a powerful Internet device, a movie and still camera, a video chat terminal, a superb gaming device, and a platform for over 200,000 apps.

Touring the iPad Exterior

The following sections briefly look at the hardware — what's on the outside.

On the top

On the top of your iPad, you'll find the headphone jack, the microphone, and the Sleep/Wake button, as shown in Figure 1-1:

✔ **On/Off, Sleep/Wake button:** This button is used to put your iPad's screen to sleep or to wake it up. It's also how you turn your iPad on or off.

When your iPad is sleeping, nothing happens if you touch its screen. To wake it up, merely press the button again or press the Home button on the front of the device.

✔ **Headphone jack:** This jack lets you plug in a pair of headphones for private listening. You can use pretty much any headphones or headset that plugs into a 3.5-mm stereo headphone jack.

✔ **Microphone:** The tiny dot at the top center of the iPad 2 is actually a microphone. (On an iPad, the mic is located on the top left.)

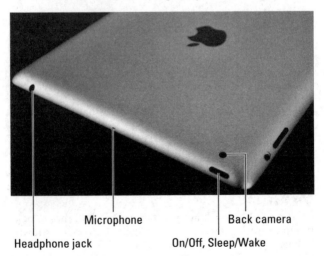

Microphone · · · · · · · · · · Back camera

Headphone jack · · · · · · · · · · On/Off, Sleep/Wake

Figure 1-1: The top side of the iPad 2.

On the bottom

On the bottom of your iPad are the speaker and the dock connector, as shown in Figure 1-2:

- ✔ **Speaker:** The speaker plays audio — music or video soundtracks — if no headset is plugged in.

- ✔ **30-pin dock connector:** This connector has two purposes. You use it to recharge your iPad's battery and to synchronize.

Built-in speaker   30-pin dock connector

Figure 1-2: The bottom side of the iPad 2.

On the sides, front, and back

On the right side of your iPad are the Volume Up/Down control and the Side switch, as shown in Figure 1-3:

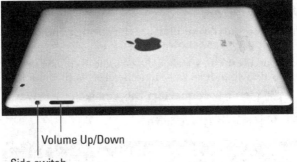

Volume Up/Down

Side switch

Figure 1-3: Right side view of the iPad.

- ✔ **Side switch:** With the iPad 2, you can set this
  switch (in Settings) as either a mute switch or a
  screen rotation lock. As a mute switch, when set
  to silent mode — the down position, with an
  orange dot visible on the switch — your iPad
  doesn't make any sound when you receive new
  mail or an alert pops up on the screen. However,
  it doesn't silence iTunes or Videos apps, nor will
  it mute games and other apps that emit noise.
  When set as a screen rotation lock, it prevents
  your screen orientation from changing
  unexpectedly.

- ✔ **Volume Up/Down control:** The Volume Up/Down
  control is a single button that's just below the
  side switch. The upper part of the button
  increases the volume; the lower part decreases it.

If you're using an iPad with 3G hardware, you may see
a Micro-SIM card tray on the left side of the device.

This tray is used to install a Micro-SIM card from your cellular provider.

On the front of your iPad, you find the following (labeled in Figure 1-4):

Touchscreen   Front camera   Application buttons

Home button

Figure 1-4: The front of the iPad 2 is a study in elegant simplicity.

- ✔ **Front Camera:** Your iPad 2 sports not one but two camera lenses — this one faces forward, allowing two-way video chatting in FaceTime.

- ✔ **Touchscreen:** The iPad has a gorgeous high-resolution color touchscreen. Try not to drool all over it.

- ✔ **Home button:** No matter what you're doing, you can press the Home button at any time to display the Home screen (refer to Figure 1-4).

- ✔ **Application buttons:** Each of the buttons (icons) shown on the screen in Figure 1-4 launches an included iPad or iPad 2 application.

On the back of your iPad 2, you'll find another camera lens (for taking video and still photos) located at the top-left corner.

Turning the iPad On and Off

After taking your iPad out of the box, press and hold the Sleep/Wake button on the upper-right edge. At first, you'll see the famous Apple logo, followed a few seconds later by a connection symbol (the USB cable leading to an iTunes icon). This is your cue to sync your iPad, which we cover in the next section.

To turn the device completely off, press and hold the Sleep/Wake button again until a red arrow appears at the top of the screen. Then drag the arrow from the left to the right with your finger. Tap Cancel at the bottom of the screen if you change your mind.

Starting to Sync

Synchronizing your iPad with your computer is a lot like syncing an iPod or iPhone with your computer. If you're an iPod or iPhone user, the process will be a familiar piece of cake. First, make sure that you've installed iTunes on your Mac or PC (if you need to download it, you can always visit www.apple.com for your own free copy). Once iTunes has been installed, follow these steps:

1. **Connect your iPad to your computer with the USB cable that came with your iPad.**

2. **Select your iPad in the iTunes sidebar.**

   You see the Welcome pane, as shown in Figure 1-5.

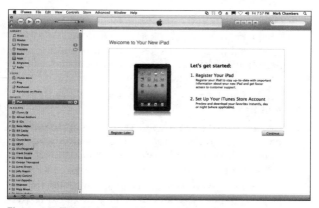

Figure 1-5: This is the first thing you see in iTunes.

3. **Click Continue.**

   iTunes presents the inevitable license agreement. After you've read the entire tome, click the I Have Read and Agree check box to select it and click Continue.

4. **Enter (or create) your Apple ID and password.**

   If you've used the iTunes Store or previously registered an Apple product, just type your ID and password. Otherwise, follow the directions for creating an Apple ID. After you enter your ID, click Continue.

5. **Enter your registration information.**

   Once you've entered everything, click Submit to register.

6. **(Optional) Set up Find My iPad.**

   This feature helps you locate your iPad if it's lost or stolen. If you do decide to use this feature, click Set up Find My iPad to display the instructions — to skip this step, click Not Now.

7. **Name your iPad by typing a name in the Name text box.**

8a. **Decide whether you want iTunes to automatically synchronize songs, videos, photos, and apps with your iPad every time you connect it to your computer.**

   • If you do want iTunes to do any of these things automatically, select the check box next to the appropriate option so that it displays a check mark and click the Done button.

- If you want to synchronize manually, make sure that all three check boxes are deselected and click Done.

8b. After you click the Done button, the Summary pane should appear.

If it doesn't, make sure that your iPad is still selected in the sidebar on the left side of the iTunes window and then click the Summary tab near the top of the window, as shown in Figure 1-6.

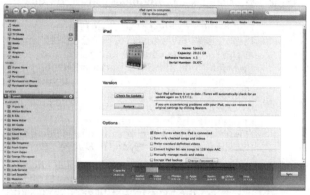

Figure 1-6: The Summary pane is pretty painless.

9. **If you want iTunes to launch automatically whenever you connect your iPad to your computer, click to put a check mark in the Open iTunes When This iPad Is Connected check box (in the Options area).**

Why might you choose not to enable this option? If you intend to connect your iPad to your computer to charge it, for example, you might not want iTunes to launch every time you connect.

If you do choose to enable the option, iTunes will launch and synchronize automatically every time you connect your iPad.

If you do select the Open iTunes When This iPad Is Connected check box but don't want your iPad to sync automatically every time it's connected, launch iTunes and choose iTunes⇨Preferences (Mac) or Edit⇨ Preferences (Windows). Click the Devices tab at the top of the window and select the Prevent iPods, iPhones, and iPads from Syncing Automatically check box. If you choose this option, you can sync your iPad by clicking the Sync or Apply button that appears in the lower-right corner of the iTunes window when your iPad is selected in the sidebar (it says "Sync" in Figure 1-6).

10. **If you want to sync only items that have check marks to the left of their names in your iTunes library, select the Sync Only Checked Songs and Videos check box.**

11. **If you want high-definition videos you import to be automatically converted into smaller standard-definition video files when you transfer them to your iPad, select the Prefer Standard Definition Videos check box.**

Standard-definition video files are significantly smaller than high-definition video files. You'll hardly notice the difference when you watch the video on your iPad, but you'll be able to have more video files on your iPad because they take up less space.

12. **If you want songs with bit rates higher than 128 kbps converted into smaller 128-kbps AAC files when you transfer them to your iPad, select the Convert Higher Bit Rate Songs to 128 kbps AAC check box.**

   A higher bit rate means that the song will have better sound quality but use a lot of storage space.

13. **If you want to turn off automatic syncing in the Music and Video panes, select the Manually Manage Music and Videos check box.**

14. **If you want to password-protect your backups (your iPad creates a backup of its contents automatically every time you sync), select the Encrypt iPad Backup check box.**

   If you do decide to encrypt your backups, click the Change Password button to enter your own password.

And, of course, if you decide to select the Prevent iPods, iPhones, and iPads from Syncing Automatically check box on iTunes Preferences' Devices tab, you can still synchronize manually by clicking the Sync button in the lower-right corner of the window.

By the way, if you've changed any sync settings since the last time you synchronized, the Sync button instead says Apply.

Synchronizing your mail accounts

Your next order of business is to sync account settings for your e-mail accounts. You do this by selecting your iPad in the sidebar on the left side of the iTunes screen. Then click the Info tab, which is to the right of the Summary tab.

In the Sync Mail Accounts section of the Info pane, you can synchronize individual accounts, as shown in Figure 1-7. Just select the appropriate check boxes.

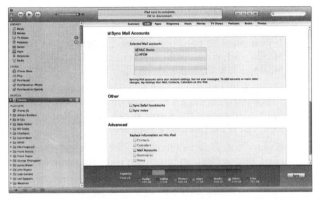

Figure 1-7: Transfer e-mail account settings to your iPad here.

The iPad syncs with the following mail programs:

  ✔ **Mac:** Apple Mail

  ✔ **PC:** Microsoft Outlook 2003, 2007 or 2010

E-mail account settings are synchronized only one way: from your computer to your iPad. If you make changes to any e-mail account settings on your iPad, the changes will *not* be synchronized back to the e-mail account on your computer.

If you sync an e-mail account and the iPad asks for a password when you send or receive mail, do this: Tap Settings on the Home screen, tap Mail, tap your e-mail account's name, and then type your password in the appropriate field.

iTunes displays a message when the syncing process finishes — at that time, you can disconnect the USB cable from your iPad and return to your mobile way of life.

Introducing the iPad Status Bar

The status bar, which is at the top of the screen, displays tiny icons that provide a variety of information about the current state of your iPad:

 Airplane mode (Wi-Fi + 3G models only): Airplane mode turns off all wireless features of your iPad and makes it possible to enjoy music or video during your flight.

3G (Wi-Fi + 3G models only): This icon informs you that the high-speed 3G data network from your wireless carrier (that's AT&T or Verizon in the United States) is available and that your iPad can connect to the Internet via 3G.

GPRS (Wi-Fi + 3G models only): This icon says that your wireless carrier's GPRS data network is available and that your iPad can use it to connect to the Internet.

EDGE (Wi-Fi + 3G models only): This icon tells you that your wireless carrier's EDGE network is available and you can use it to connect to the Internet.

 Wi-Fi: If you see the Wi-Fi icon, it means your iPad is connected to the Internet over a Wi-Fi network. The more semicircular lines you see (up to three), the stronger the Wi-Fi signal.

 Activity: This icon tells you that some network or other activity is occurring, such as over-the-air synchronization, sending or receiving e-mail, or loading a Web page.

 VPN: This icon shows that you are connected to a virtual private network (VPN).

 Lock: This icon tells you when your iPad is locked.

 Play: This icon informs you that a song is currently playing.

 Bluetooth: This icon indicates the state of your iPad's Bluetooth connection. If the icon is gray (as shown on the right in the picture in the margin), Bluetooth is turned on but no device is connected. If the icon is white (as shown on the left in the picture in the margin), Bluetooth is on and one or more devices are connected. If you don't see a Bluetooth icon at all, Bluetooth is turned off.

 Screen orientation lock: This icon appears when the Screen Rotation Lock is engaged.

Battery: This icon reflects the level of your battery's charge.

Home Sweet Home Screen

The Home screen offers numerous icons by default, each representing a different built-in application or function. We merely provide brief descriptions here.

To get to your Home screen, tap the Home button. If your iPad is asleep when you tap, the unlock screen appears. After it is unlocked, you see whichever page was on the screen when it went to sleep. If it wasn't the Home screen, tap the Home button again.

Three steps let you rearrange icons on your iPad:

1. **Press and hold any icon until all the icons begin to "wiggle."**

2. **Drag the icons around until you're happy with their positions.**

3. **Press the Home button to save your arrangement and stop the "wiggling."**

If you haven't rearranged your icons, you see the following applications on your Home screen, starting at the top left:

✔ **Calendar:** No matter what calendar program you prefer on your PC or Mac (as long as it's iCal, Microsoft Entourage, or Microsoft Outlook), you can synchronize events and alerts between your computer and your iPad.

✔ **Contacts:** This handy app contains information about the people you know. Like the Calendar app, it synchronizes with the contacts app on your Mac or PC (again, as long as it's iCal,

Microsoft Entourage, or Microsoft Outlook), and you can synchronize contacts between your computer and your iPad.

✔ **Notes:** This program enables you to type notes while you're out and about. You can send the notes to yourself or to anyone else through e-mail, or just save them on your iPad until you need them.

✔ **Maps:** This application is among our favorites. View street maps or satellite imagery of locations around the globe, or ask for directions, traffic conditions, or even the location of a nearby pizza joint.

✔ **Videos:** This handy app is the repository for your movies, TV shows, and music videos. You add videos via iTunes on your Mac or PC, or by purchasing them from the iTunes Store using the iTunes app on your iPad.

✔ **YouTube:** This application lets you watch videos from the popular YouTube Web site. You can search for a particular video or browse through thousands of offerings. It's a great way to waste a lot of time.

✔ **iTunes:** Tap this puppy to purchase music, movies, TV shows, audiobooks, and more, and also download free podcasts and courses from iTunes U.

✔ **App Store:** This icon enables you to connect to and search the iTunes App Store for iPad applications that you can purchase or download free over a Wi-Fi or cellular data network connection.

- ✔ **Game Center:** Apple's social networking app for game enthusiasts. Compare achievements, boast of your conquests and high scores, or challenge your friends to battle.

- ✔ **FaceTime:** On an iPad 2, tap this icon to start a two-way video chat with a Mac computer, another iPad 2, or an iPhone 4.

- ✔ **Camera:** On an iPad 2, this icon opens the iPad 2 Camera application, which lets you take still photographs and video clips.

- ✔ **Photo Booth:** Remember the coin-operated photo booth at arcades and carnivals? This iPad 2 application allows you to take photos with all sorts of special effects (favorites are Thermal Camera and Squeeze). The perfect party application!

- ✔ **Settings:** This is where you change settings for your iPad and its apps.

- ✔ **Safari:** Safari is your Web browser. If you're a Mac user, you know that already. If you're a Windows user who hasn't already discovered the wonderful Safari for Windows, think Internet Explorer on steroids.

- ✔ **Mail:** This application lets you send and receive e-mail with most POP3 and IMAP e-mail systems and, if you work for a company that grants permission, Microsoft Exchange, too.

- ✔ **Photos:** This application is the iPad's terrific photo manager. You can view pictures that you've taken (with your iPad 2) or transferred from your computer, camera, or SD card reader (using the

optional Camera Connection Kit). You can zoom
in or out, create slideshows, e-mail photos to
friends, and much more.

✔ **iPod:** Last but not least, this icon unleashes all the
power of an iPod right on your iPad, so you can
listen to music or podcasts.

Mastering Multitouch

With very few exceptions, until the iPad came along,
most every computer known to mankind has had a
physical mouse and a typewriter-style QWERTY keyboard to help you accomplish most of the things you
can do on a computer. (The term *QWERTY* is derived
from the first six letters on any standard typewriter or
computer keyboard.)

The iPad, like the iPhone, dispenses with a physical
mouse and keyboard in favor of a *multitouch display.*
This beautiful and responsive finger-controlled screen
is at the heart of the many things you do on the iPad.

In the following sections, you discover how to move
around the multitouch interface with ease.

Training your digits

Rice Krispies have Snap! Crackle! Pop! Apple's response
for the iPad is Tap! Flick! and Pinch! (Yikes, another ad
comparison!) Oh yeah, and drag.

Fortunately, tapping, flicking, pinching, and dragging
are not challenging gestures, so you can master many
of the iPad's features in no time:

✔ **Tap:** Tapping serves multiple purposes. Tap an
icon to open an application from the Home

screen. Tap to start playing a song or to choose the photo album you want to look through. Sometimes, you double-tap (tapping twice in rapid succession), which has the effect of zooming in (or out) of Web pages, maps, and e-mails.

✔ **Flick:** Flicking is just what it sounds like. A flick of the finger on the screen itself lets you quickly scroll through lists of songs, e-mails, and picture thumbnails. Tap on the screen to stop scrolling, or merely wait for the scrolling list to stop.

✔ **Pinch/spread:** Place two fingers on the edges of a Web page or map or picture, and then spread your fingers apart to enlarge the images. Or, pinch your fingers together to make the map or picture smaller. Pinching and spreading (*unpinching*) are cool gestures that are easy to master and sure to wow an audience.

✔ **Drag:** Here's where you slowly press your finger against the touchscreen without lifting it. You might drag to move around a Web page or map that's too large for the iPad's display area.

Navigating beyond the Home screen

The Home screen is not the only screen of icons on your tablet. After you start adding apps from the iTunes App Store, you may see two or more tiny dots between the Safari, Mail, Photos, and iPod icons and the row of icons directly above them, plus a tiny Spotlight search magnifying glass to the left of the dots. Those dots denote additional screens, each containing up to 20 additional icons, not counting the four to six separate icons that are docked at the bottom of each of these Home screens.

To navigate between screens, either flick your finger from right to left or left to right across the middle of the screen, or tap directly on the dots. You can also drag your finger in either horizontal direction to get to a different screen.

Part II

The iPad Online

he Apple Safari Web browser is a major reason the Net on the iPad is very much like the Net you've come to expect on a more traditional computer. We think Safari is one of the very best Web browsers in the business.

Going on Safari

Surfing the Web begins with a Web address, of course. When you start by tapping the address field in iPad's Safari, the virtual keyboard appears. Here are a few tips for using the keyboard in Safari:

▸   ✔ Because so many Web addresses end with the suffix `.com` (pronounced *dot com*), the virtual

keyboard has a dedicated .com key. For other
common Web suffixes — `.edu`, `.net`, and `.org` —
press and hold the .com key and choose the rele-
vant domain type.

✔ Of equal importance, both the period (.) and the
slash (/) are on the virtual keyboard because you
frequently use them when you enter Web
addresses.

✔ The moment you tap a single letter, you see a list
of Web addresses that match those letters. For
example, if you tap the letter *E* (as in the example
shown in Figure 2-1), you see Web listings for
EarthLink, eBay, and others. Tapping *U* or *H*
instead may display listings for *USA TODAY* or the
Houston Chronicle.

The iPad has two ways to determine Web sites to suggest when you tap certain letters:

✔ **Bookmarks:** One method is the Web sites you
already bookmarked from the Safari or Internet
Explorer browsers on your computer.

✔ **History:** The second method iPad uses when
suggesting Web sites when you tap a particular
letter is to suggest sites from the History list —
those cyberdestinations where you recently hung
your hat.

You might as well open your first Web page now — and
it's a full *HTML* page, to borrow from techie lingo:

1. **Tap the Safari icon docked at the bottom of the
   Home screen.**

   It's another member of the Fantastic Four (along
   with Mail, Photos, and iPod).

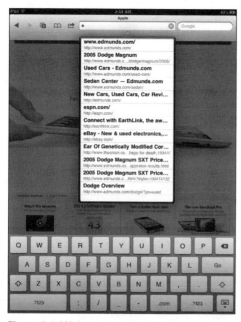

Figure 2-1: Web pages that match your search letter.

2. Tap the Web address field.

3. Begin typing the Web address on the virtual keyboard that slides up from the bottom of the screen.

4. **Do one of the following:**

   a. To accept one of the bookmarked (or other) sites that show up on the list, merely tap the name.

      Safari automatically fills in the address and takes you where you want to go.

   b. Keep tapping the proper keyboard characters until you enter the complete Web address for the site you have in mind. Next tap the Go key found on the right side of the keyboard.

It's not necessary to type **www** at the beginning of a Web address. So, if you want to visit www.theonion.com (for example), typing **theonion.com** is sufficient to transport you to the humor site. For that matter, it even works if you type **theonion** without the .com.

After the page has loaded, tap a link to follow it — just like you would click the link with your computer's mouse.

Getting the Mail Through

The built-in Mail application on the iPad is designed to not only send and receive text e-mail messages but also to handle rich HTML e-mail messages — formatted with font and type styles and embedded graphics. If someone sends you mail with a picture, it's visible right in the body of the message.

Furthermore, your iPad can read several types of file attachments, including (but not limited to) PDFs, JPG images, Microsoft Word documents, PowerPoint slides, Excel spreadsheets, and stuff produced through Apple's iWork software. Better still, all this sending and receiving of text, graphics, and documents can happen in the background so that you can surf the Web or play a game while your iPad quietly and efficiently handles your e-mail behind the scenes.

Sending an all-text message

To compose a new e-mail message, tap Mail on the Home screen. What you see next depends on how you're holding your iPad. In landscape mode (Figure 2-2), your e-mail accounts or e-mail folders are listed in a panel along the left side of screen, with the actual message filling the larger window on the right.

Depending on the last time the mail application was open, you may alternatively see previews of the actual messages in your inbox in the left panel. Previews show the name of the sender, the subject header, and the first two lines of the message. (In Settings, you can change the number of lines shown in the preview from 1 to 5. Or, you can show no preview lines.)

When you hold the iPad in portrait mode, the last incoming message fills the entire screen. Figure 2-3 shows this view. You have to tap an Inbox button (in

the upper-left corner of the screen) to summon a panel
that shows other accounts or message previews. These
overlay the message that otherwise fills the screen.

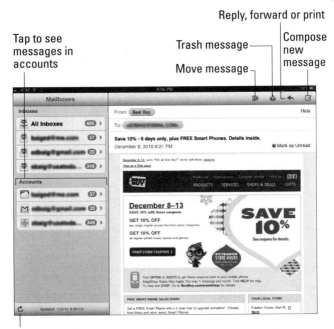

Reply, forward or print

Tap to see
messages in
accounts

Trash message

Compose
new
message

Move message

Check for new messages

Figure 2-2: When holding the iPad sideways, Mail looks like this.

Figure 2-3: When holding the iPad in portrait mode, the message fills the screen.

Now, to create a new message, follow these steps:

1. **Tap the Compose New Message button (refer to Figure 2-2).**

    A screen like the one shown in Figure 2-4 appears.

Figure 2-4: The New Message screen appears, ready for you to start typing the recipient's name.

2. **Type the names or e-mail addresses of the recipients in the To field, or tap the + button to the right of the To field to choose a contact or contacts from your iPad's contacts list.**

3. **(Optional) Tap the field labeled Cc/Bcc, From.**

   Doing so breaks them out into separate Cc, Bcc, and From fields.

   The Cc/Bcc label stands for *carbon copy/blind carbon copy*. Carbon copy is kind of an FYI to a recipient. It's like saying, "We figure you'd appreciate knowing this but you don't need to respond."

   When using Bcc, you can include a recipient on the message but other recipients can't see that this recipient has been included. It's great for those secret agent e-mails! Tap the respective Cc or Bcc field to type names. Or, tap the + symbol that appears in those fields to add a contact.

4. **(Optional) If you tap From, you can choose to send the message from any of your e-mail accounts on the fly, assuming, of course, that you have more than one account set up on the iPad.**

   If you start typing an e-mail address, e-mail addresses that match what you typed appear in a list below the To or Cc field. If the correct one is in the list, tap it to use it.

5. **Type a subject in the Subject field.**

The subject is optional, but it's considered poor form to send an e-mail message without one.

6. **Type your message in the message area.**

The message area is immediately below the Subject field. You have ample space to get your message across.

7. **Tap the Send button in the upper-right corner of the screen.**

Your message wings its way to its recipients almost immediately. If you aren't in range of a Wi-Fi network or the AT&T EDGE or 3G data network when you tap Send, the message is sent the next time you're in range of one of these networks.

 Apple includes a bunch of landscape-orientation keyboards in various applications, including Mail. When you rotate the iPad to its side, you can compose a new message using a wider-format virtual keyboard.

Sending a photo with a text message

Sometimes a picture is worth a thousand words. When that's the case, here's how to send an e-mail message with a photo enclosed:

1. **Tap the Photos icon on the Home screen.**

2. **Find the photo you want to send.**

3. **Tap the button that looks like a little rectangle with a curved arrow springing out of it in the upper-right corner of the screen.**

4. **Tap the Email Photo button.**

   An e-mail message appears on-screen with the photo already attached. In fact, the image appears to be embedded in the body of the message, but the recipient receives it as a regular e-mail attachment.

5. **Address the message and type whatever text you like, as you did for an all-text message in the preceding section, and then tap the Send button.**

Reading messages

To read your mail, tap the Mail icon on the Home screen. Remember that what appears on the screen depends on whether you're holding the iPad in portrait or landscape mode, and what was on the screen the last time you opened the Mail application. Held in land-scape mode, you'll see the All Inboxes at the top of the Inboxes section (refer to Figure 2-2), which as its name suggests is a repository for all the messages across all your accounts. The number to the right of All Inboxes should match the number on the Mail icon on your Home page. Again, it's the cumulative tally of unread messages across all your accounts.

Below the All Inboxes listing are the inboxes for your individual accounts. The tally this time is only for the unread messages in those accounts. If you tap the list-ings here, you'll see any subfolders for each individual account (Drafts, Sent Mail, Trash, and so on). Messages are displayed in threads or conversations making them easy to follow. Of course, you can still view accounts individually. Follow these steps to read your e-mail:

1. **If the e-mail mailbox you want to see isn't front and center, tap the Accounts button in the upper-left corner of the screen to summon the appropriate one.**

   Again, this button may say Inbox or some other folder name, and it may say the name of the e-mail account that is currently open. Within an e-mail account, you can see the number of unread messages in each mailbox.

2. **(Optional) Tap the Check for New Messages icon (refer to Figure 2-2) to summon new messages.**

3. **Tap one of the inboxes or accounts to check for any new messages within those mailboxes. To summon the unified inbox, tap All Inboxes instead.**

   If a blue dot appears next to a message, it means that the message has not been read. When you open a mailbox by tapping it, the iPad displays the number of "recent" messages that you specify in Settings — 50 by default, though you can display up to 200. To see more than the number you specified, tap Load Additional Messages.

4. **Tap a message to read it.**

   When a message is on the screen, the buttons for managing incoming messages appear at the top of the screen, most of which you're already familiar with. If you're holding the iPad in portrait mode, you'll see up/down arrows that correspond to the next or previous message.

5. **In landscape mode (and from within an account),
tap a preview listing to the left of a message to
read the next or previous message or any other
visible message on the list. Scroll up or down to
find other messages you may want to read.**

   A number next to one of the previews indicates
   the number of related messages in a conversation
   or *thread*.

Under a thread, only the first message of the conversation displays in the inbox. Tap that message to reveal
the entire back and forth. You can turn message thread-
ing off by choosing Settings➪Mail, Contacts, Calendars.

Chatting with FaceTime

One of the iPad 2's great new features is FaceTime, the
app that allows you to video chat with other FaceTime
users over a WiFi link.

You need a WiFi connection to use FaceTime —
a 3G cellular connection will not work — and
the other person will need a Mac computer,
iPad 2, or iPhone 4 with FaceTime installed.

The first time you use FaceTime, you must enter your
Apple ID and your e-mail address (other people will use
your e-mail address to call you using FaceTime).

After you sign in, follow these steps to make a call:

1. **Tap a contact from the list.**

   FaceTime displays your Contacts list by default,
   but there are other methods of selecting someone
   to call. To display a list of recent calls, tap the

Recent icon. You can also display a list of your favorite FaceTime callers by tapping the Favorites icon — to add someone as a favorite, tap the Add button (which carries a plus sign) at the top of the list.

2. **Once the call is accepted, you'll see video from the caller's location.**

   Speak normally, and your caller should have no problem hearing you.

3. **(Optional) During the call, switch between front and back cameras by tapping the Camera Switch icon.**

   You can use either camera with FaceTime — send video of yourself with the front camera, or share your surroundings while you talk using the back camera.

4. **(Optional) To turn off audio from your side of the call, tap the Mute icon.**

   You can still hear audio from the caller's side of the conversation. Tap the Mute icon again to turn your microphone back on.

   Press the Home button during a call, and you can run another app! You won't see the video, of course, but you can continue talking. Once you're done with the other application, tap the green bar at the top of the window to return to FaceTime.

5. **To hang up and end the call, tap the End icon.**

If someone calls you with FaceTime, your iPad 2 will notify you with a message, and you can choose to accept or dismiss the call.

Maps Are Where It's At

The Maps feature was one of the sleeper hits of the iPhone because it's so darn handy. With Maps, you can quickly and easily discover exactly where you are, find nearby restaurants and businesses, get turn-by-turn driving instructions from any address to any other address, and see real-time traffic information and a photographic street view of many locations as well.

To download and use apps, make sure you're connected to the Internet via either Wi-Fi or 3G.

Finding a person, place, or thing

To find a person, place, or thing with Maps, tap the Maps icon on the Home page, then follow these steps:

1. **Tap the Search field in the upper-right corner of the screen to make the keyboard appear.**

2. **Now type what you're looking for.**

   You can search for addresses, zip codes, intersections, towns, landmarks, and businesses by category and by name, or combinations, such as New York, NY 10022, pizza 60645, or Auditorium Shores Austin TX.

3. **(Optional) If the letters you type match names in your Contacts list, the matching contacts appear in a list below the Search field. Tap a name to see a map of that contact's location.**

   Maps is smart about it, too; it displays only the names of contacts that have a street address.

4. **When you finish typing, tap Search.**

   After a few seconds, a map appears. If you searched for a single location, it is marked with a single pushpin. If you searched for a category (pizza 60645, for example), you see multiple pushpins, one for each matching location.

Socializing with Social Media Apps

Your iPad doesn't include any specific social media apps right out of the box, but you can add free client apps for the major social media networks including Facebook, Myspace, Twitter, and the new kid on the block, Apple's Game Center.

That's the good news. The bad news is that as of this writing, only Game Center and Twitter offer client apps that run natively on the iPad. However, we are certain they'll get around to releasing bigger, better, iPad-friendly apps soon.

Note that you don't necessarily need an app to participate in social networking. The following three networks can be fully utilized using Safari on your iPad. And, unlike the iPhone where the Safari experience was hampered by the tiny screen and keyboard, all three Web sites are eminently usable on your iPad. So, if you want to check them out and don't feel like downloading their apps, here are their addresses:

- ✔ Facebook: www.facebook.com
- ✔ Myspace: www.myspace.com
- ✔ Twitter: http://twitter.com

Part III

The iPad at Play

* *

In This Part

▶ Browsing for apps

▶ Getting an app on your iPad

▶ Using the iPad as an iPod

▶ Finding and playing video

▶ Taking photos

▶ Curling up with a good book

* *

One of the best things about the iPad these days is that you can download and install apps created by third parties, which is to say apps not created by Apple (the first party) or you (the second party). You'll find a couple hundred thousand apps in the iTunes App Store — that should keep you busy for a few days, at least.

The Magic of the Apps

Apps enable you to use your iPad as a game console, a streaming Netflix player, a recipe finder, a sketchbook, and much, much more. You can run three different categories of apps on your iPad:

- ✔ **Apps made exclusively for the iPad:** This is the newest kind, so you find fewer of these than the other two types.

- ✔ **Apps made to work properly on an iPad, iPhone, or iPod touch:** This type of app can run on any of the three devices at full resolution. For the iPhone and iPod touch, full resolution is 320 x 480 pixels; for the iPad, it's 1024 x 768 pixels.

- ✔ **Apps made for the iPhone and iPod touch:** These apps run on your iPad but only at iPhone/iPod touch resolution (320 x 480) rather than the full resolution of your iPad (1024 x 768).

You can double the size of an iPhone/iPod touch app by tapping the little 2x button in the lower-right corner of the screen; to return it to its native size, tap the 1x button.

You can obtain and install apps for your iPad in two ways:

- ✔ On your computer
- ✔ On your iPad

To use the App Store on your iPad, it must be connected to the Internet. And, if you download an app on your computer, it isn't available on your iPad until you sync it with your computer.

But before you can use the App Store on your iPad or your computer, you first need an iTunes Store account. If you don't already have one, launch iTunes on your computer, click Sign In near the upper-right corner of the iTunes window, click Create New Account, and then follow the on-screen instructions.

Finding an app

You can shop for apps, purchase them, and download them automatically using the App Store on your iPad — the icon for the App Store appears on the Home screen on your iPad. However, you can also use your computer to find cool iPad apps using iTunes. Follow these steps within iTunes:

1. **Launch iTunes.**

2. **Click the iTunes Store link in the sidebar on the left.**

3. **Click the App Store link at the top of the window, then choose the category from the pop-up menu that appears.**

   The iTunes App Store appears, as shown in Figure 3-1.

Downloading an app to your computer

When you find an application to try, click its Free App or Buy App button. After you do so, you have to log on to your iTunes Store account, even if the app is free. To download an application to your iPad, follow these steps:

1. **Click the price button near the top of its detail screen.**

2. **When prompted, type your iTunes Store account password.**

3. **After the application has been downloaded to your computer, connect your iPad and allow it to sync.**

iPad tab

iTunes App Store menu   Search iTunes Store

iTunes Store link   Scroll bar

Figure 3-1: The iTunes App Store, in all its glory.

When you buy an application through the iPad's built-in App Store, the application is automatically installed on your iPad, but it isn't copied to your iTunes library on your Mac or PC until your next sync.

After you pay for an app, you can download it again if you need to — from iTunes on your computer or the App Store app on your iPad — and you don't have to pay for it again.

Playing the iPod inside Your iPad

To use your iPad as an iPod, tap the iPod icon on the right side of the dock at the bottom of the screen (unless you've moved it elsewhere).

Here's a quick overview of what you see when the iPod app starts up:

- ✔ **Audio library:** Along the left side of the screen, you'll see your iPad audio library, which contains all the music, podcasts, audiobooks, and playlists you've synced with or purchased on your iPad. Tap Music.

  Along the right side of the screen, running from top to bottom, you see the letters of the alphabet from A to Z (unless you're looking at the Genres tab, which doesn't need them). Tap one to jump to that letter instantly when you're browsing Songs, Artists, Albums, or Composers.

- ✔ **Player controls:** At the top of the screen, from left to right, you can see the volume control, the Rewind/Previous Track button, the Play/Pause button, the Fast Forward/Next Track button, and the Search field.

- ✔ **Playlist and tab navigation:** At the bottom of the screen, from left to right, you can see a plus sign for adding new playlists, the Genius symbol for creating Genius playlists, and five tabs: Songs, Artists, Albums, Genres, and Composers.

Figure 3-2 shows all of these features.

Library — Play/Pause button — Alphabet

Rewind/Previous Track button — Fast Forward/Next Track button

Volume control — Search field

Genius Playlist — Tabs — Scrubber bar and Playhead

New Playlist

Figure 3-2: These components are what you'll find on the iPod app's main screen.

iTunes includes a *Home Sharing* feature, which allows you to play music, movies, and TV shows from your computer's iTunes library on your iPad. Both your computer and iPad must be using the same WiFi network. Within iTunes, click Advanced➪Turn on Home Sharing. On your iPad, open Settings and tap iPod, then enter the same Apple ID and password as you entered on your computer. Within the iPod app, you can now tap the Library item in the list and enjoy your stuff wirelessly!

Finding Stuff to Watch

You have a couple of ways to find and watch videos on your iPad. You can fetch all sorts of fare from the iTunes Store, whose virtual doors you can open directly from the iPad.

Or, you can sync content that already resides on your PC or Mac. The videos you can watch on the iPad generally fall into one of the following categories:

✓ **Movies, TV shows, and music videos that you purchase or fetch free in the iTunes Store:** You can watch these by tapping the Videos icon on the Home screen.

The iTunes Store features dedicated sections for purchasing or renting episodes of TV shows, as shown in Figure 3-3, and for buying or renting movies.

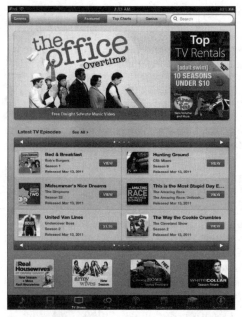

Figure 3-3: Buying and watching TV on the iPad.

The typical price is $1.99 to pick up a single episode of a popular TV show in standard definition or $2.99 for high-def versions. You can rent certain shows commercial free for 99 cents. You can even purchase a complete season of a favorite show.

Feature films fetch prices from $9.99 to $19.99.

As shown in Figure 3-4, by tapping a movie listing in iTunes, you can generally watch a trailer before buying (or renting) and check out additional tidbits: plot summary, credits, reviews, and customer ratings, as well as other movies that appealed to the buyer of this one. And you can search films by genre or top charts (the ones other people are buying or renting), or rely on the Apple Genius feature for recommendations based on stuff you've already watched. (Genius works for movies and TV much the way it works for music.)

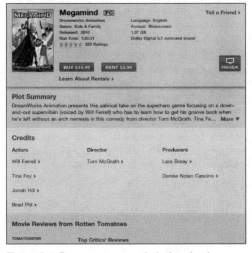

Figure 3-4: Bone up on a movie before buying or renting it.

- ✔ **The boatload of video podcasts, just about all of them free, featured in the iTunes Store:** Podcasts started out as another form of Internet radio, although instead of listening to live streams, you download files onto your computer or iPod to take in at your leisure. You can still find lots of audio podcasts, but the focus here is on video. You can watch free episodes that cover Sesame Street videos, sports programming, investing strategies, political shows (across the ideological spectrum), and so much more.

- ✔ **Videos that play via entertainment apps:** For example, Netflix offers an app that enables you to use your Netflix subscription, if you have one, to stream video on your iPad. Similarly, the ABC television network offers an appealing app so that you can catch up on its shows on your iPad.

- ✔ **Take a seminar at Harvard, Stanford, or numerous other prestigious institutions:** iTunes University boasts more than 250,000 free lectures from around the world, many of them videos. Better yet, you get no grades, and you don't have to apply for admission, write an essay, or do homework. Figure 3-5 shows the iTunes U description for Open University's *The Galapagos*.

- ✔ **Homegrown videos from the popular YouTube Internet site:** Apple obviously thinks highly of YouTube because it devoted a dedicated Home screen icon to the site.

Figure 3-5: Get smart. iTunes University offers a slew of lectures on diverse topics.

✔ **The movies you've created in iMovie software or other software on the Mac or, for that matter, other programs on the PC:** Plus all the other videos that you may have downloaded from the Internet.

You may have to prepare these videos so that they'll play on your iPad. To do so, highlight the video in question after it resides in your iTunes library. Go to the Advanced menu in iTunes, and click Create iPad or Apple TV Version. Alas, this doesn't work for all the video content you download off the Internet, including video files in the AVI, DivX, MKV, and Xvid formats. You need help transferring these formats to iTunes and converting them to iPad-friendly formats from other software programs added to your PC or Mac.

Playing Video

Now that you know what you want to watch, here's how to watch it:

1. **On the Home screen, tap the Videos icon.**

   Videos stored on your iPad are segregated by category — Movies, Rented Movies, TV Shows, Podcasts, Music Videos, and iTunes U. For each category, you see the program's poster art. Categories such as Rented Movies, Podcasts, and iTunes U only appear if you have that type of content loaded on the machine.

2. **At the top of the screen, select the tab that corresponds to the type of video you want to watch.**

3. **Tap the poster that represents the movie, TV show, or other video you want to watch.**

   You see a full description of the movie you want to watch, along with a listing of cast and filmmakers.

Tap the Chapters tab to browse the chapters. You see thumbnail images and the length of the chapter. Tap the Info tab to return to a description.

4. **To start playing a movie (or resume playing from where you left off), tap the Play button, labeled in Figure 3-6.**

Play movie

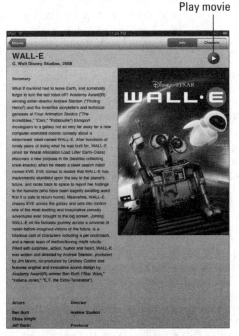

Figure 3-6: Getting a description of the movie you're about to watch.

If you go to Settings from the Home screen and tap Video, you can change the default setting to start playing from where you left off to playing from the beginning.

5. **(Optional) Rotate your iPad to landscape mode to maximize a movie's display.**

    If you hold the iPad in portrait mode, you see black bars on top of and below the screen where the movie is playing. Those bars remain when you rotate the device to its side, but the iPad is now playing the film in a wide-screen mode.

The iPad doesn't give you a full high-definition presentation because that requires 1280-x-720-pixel resolution and the iPad's screen is 1024 x 768, meaning that it is scaled down slightly.

 By using an Apple Digital AV Adapter and an HDMI cable, your iPad 2 can display the same video on both the built-in screen and a TV with an HDMI port. Tap the Settings icon on the Home screen, and then tap Video to configure your iPad for widescreen display on your TV.

Shooting Photos and Video

You can use the Camera app to take still photos and video using either of your iPad 2's cameras. Tap the Camera icon, and you'll see a real-time display — to switch cameras between front and back, tap the Switch icon at the upper-right corner of the screen. (You can change the camera's orientation by simply rotating your iPad 2.) To switch between still photos and video, tap the Photo/Video icon at the lower right of the screen.

As you probably already know, digital video takes a lot of room on your iPad 2, so be selective when shooting video.

When you're ready to shoot, tap the Camera button at the bottom center of the screen. If you're shooting video, tap the Camera button again to stop recording. To review your photos and video clips, tap the Review thumbnail at the bottom left of the screen — you can print and e-mail your handiwork, as well as use photos as wallpaper.

While reviewing your photos, tap the Slideshow button at the top of the screen for an instant professional-looking slideshow.

To add a little spice and special effects to your still photos, tap the Photo Booth icon on your iPad 2's Home screen. You can choose from any of eight different effects for your images — again, you can also switch between the front and back cameras. Tap the Camera button to shoot some out-of-this-world photos.

Just Browsing: iBookstore

To start reading electronic books on your iPad, you have to fetch the iBooks app in the App Store. As you might imagine, the app is free, and it comes with access to Apple's brand-new iBookstore.

The top half of the screen shows ever-changing ads for books that fit a chosen category. But you can also browse Recent Releases in the particular category you have in mind. The left- and right-pointing arrows indicate more recent releases to peek at. Or tap See All for many more selections.

To choose another category of books, tap the Categories button; you may have to scroll to see the bottom of the list. Figure 3-7 illustrates a typical category display.

Figure 3-7: The featured page for the Humor category.

Now look at the bottom of the screen. You see the following icons:

- **Featured:** Featured works are the books being promoted in the store. These may include popular titles from Oprah's Book Club or an author spotlight from the likes of Twilight writer Stephenie Meyer.

- **NYTimes:** Short for *The New York Times,* of course. These books made the newspaper's famous bestsellers lists, which are divided into fiction and nonfiction works.

- **Top Charts:** Here Apple is showing you the most popular books in the iBookstore. You'll find a list for Top Paid Books and Top Free Books.

- **Browse:** Tap this icon to search the store in a convenient list form (by authors or categories).

- **Purchases:** Tapping here shows you the books you've already bought.

Buying a Book from the iBookstore

When you are ready to purchase a book, here's how to do so:

1. **Tap the price shown in the gray button on the book's information page.**

   Upon doing so, the dollar amount disappears and the button becomes green and carries a Buy Book label. If you tap a free book instead, the button is labeled Get Book.

2. **Tap the Buy Book/Get Book button.**

3. **Enter your iTunes password to proceed with the transaction.**

   The book appears on your bookshelf in an instant, ready for you to tap it and start reading.

Reading a Book

To start reading a book, tap it. The book leaps off the shelf, and at the same time, it opens to either the beginning of the book or the place where you left off.

From the title page, you can appreciate the color and beauty of Apple's app as well as the navigation tools, shown in Figure 3-8.

 You can take advantage of the iPad's VoiceOver feature to have the iPad read to you aloud. It may not be quite like having Mom or Dad read you to sleep, but it can be a potential godsend to those of you with impaired vision.

Table of Contents   Brightness   Text Size and Fonts   Search

Slider

Figure 3-8: Books on the iPad offer handy reading and navigation tools.